# Country, Cat City, Cat

**FOUR WINDS PRESS    NEW YORK**

# Country, Cat City, Cat

BY DAVID KHERDIAN

Woodcuts by Nonny Hogrogian

Library of Congress Cataloging in Publication Data
Kherdian, David.
 Country, cat, city, cat.
 SUMMARY: Poems about cats, the city, and the
country.
 1. Cats—Juvenile poetry.   2. City and town life—
Juvenile poetry.   3. Country life—Juvenile poetry.
[1. Cats—Poetry.   2. City and town life—Poetry.
3. Country life—Poetry.   4. American poetry]
I. Hogrogian, Nonny.   II. Title.
PZ8.3.K5Co        811'.5'4        77–2555
ISBN 0–590–07482–2

Published by Four Winds Press
A Division of Scholastic Magazines, Inc., New York, N.Y.
Copyright © 1978 by David Kherdian and Nonny H. Kherdian
All rights reserved
Printed in the United States of America
Library of Congress Catalog Card Number: 77–2555

1   2   3   4   5        81   80   79   78   77

For reprint permission, grateful acknowledgment is made to:

Giligia Press for "butterflies roost" from *On the Death of My Father and Other Poems*, copyright © 1970 by David Kherdian.

*Images* for "The White Daisies" and "Higher and Lower Mathematics."

The Macmillan Company for the first haiku in "Winter News," "From the Window," "Hey Nonny," and "April Winter," from *The Nonny Poems* by David Kherdian, copyright © 1974 by David Kherdian.

*The Margarine Maypole Orangoutang Express* for "Victims 3 Cat 0" and "Opening the Door and Entering the Barnyard, etc."

Overlook Press for "Stillness" (originally appeared in *Adoyl* as 20:XII:72), "Almost," "Lyme, New Hampshire," "Cat" (originally appeared in *Adoyl* as 16:IV:73), "Opening the Door on the 18th of January, Late in the Evening, To Let the Cat In," "Just Now" (originally appeared in *Adoyl* as 26:VIII:73), all from *Any Day of Your Life*, copyright © 1975 by David Kherdian.

FOR MISSAK, WHO ELSE

# COUNTRY, CAT

OPENING THE DOOR
ON THE 18TH OF JANUARY,
LATE IN THE EVENING,
TO LET THE CAT IN

as the moon glides through
streaking clouds

the cat with frightened
tail

sniffs and enters
his only home

WINTER NEWS

chickadees
round suet balls
winter has come

•

the winter fly
at the screen
wants to come in

•

the sparrows have
been ice-skating
on the bird bath again

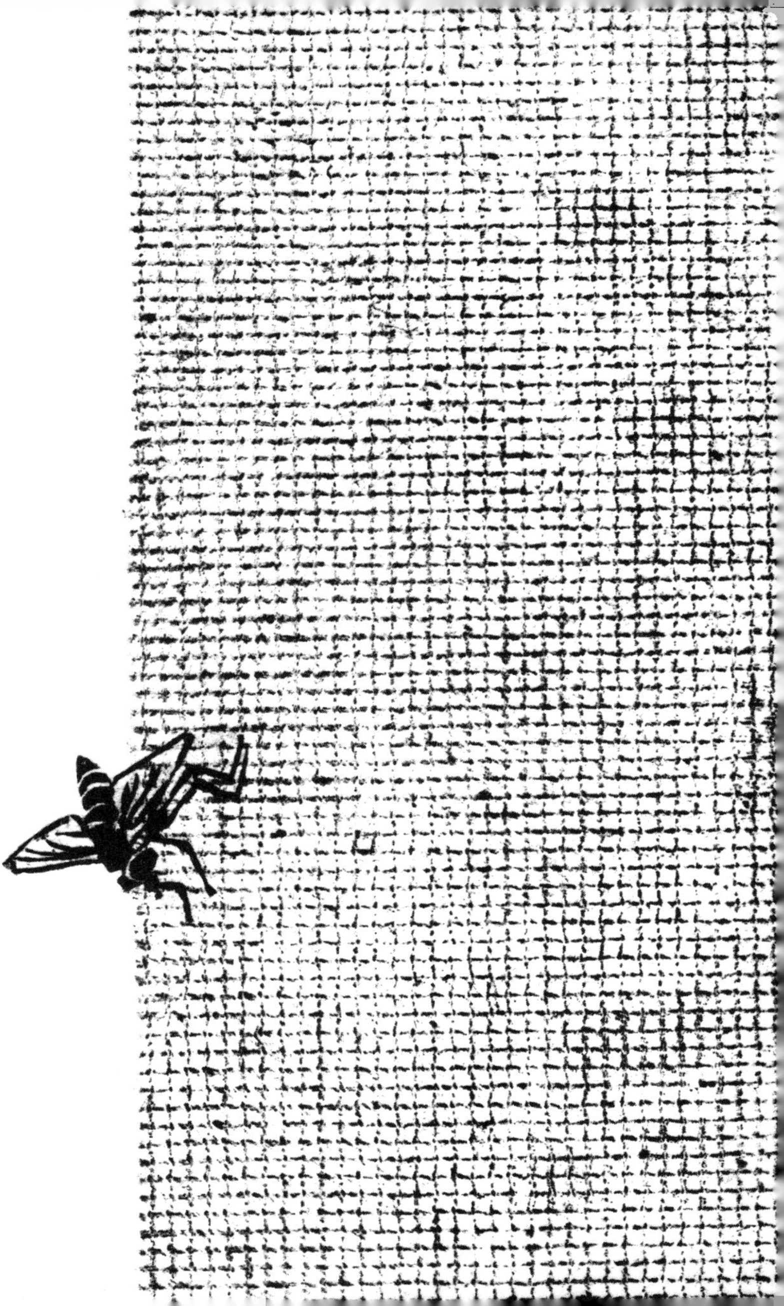

## FROM THE WINDOW

pushing heavy
breasted through
the snow
hurriedly pecking
at fallen seeds
he makes a
zigzag trail through
the half-buried
prickly pine

now
looking up
he's gone
the only ruby-
crowned kinglet
this winter
hurrah!

stillness
snowfall
in the valley
across the mountain
a bird flies
in the cathedral
of the wind

HEY NONNY

the chickadee
must have seen
a seed
in the snow
down
from the branch
to go neck
deep into the
soft white
of it
and now
the snow is
falling
on his head

ALMOST

the woodpecker
hammers
on the
lilac bush
out for
branch lice
gnats and goodies
at the end
of winter
beside the
abandoned feeder:
the soft colors
of spring
in the air
and on the way

6113

LYME, NEW HAMPSHIRE

the flea-bitten dog
in front of the
ramshackle garage
in the aging New
England village
(on the last day
of March)

sits alone in the
new dust of spring

VICTIMS 3    CAT 0

Missak is dancing
beyond the barn—
a little early
spring voodoo
for the baby squirrels
mice and chipmunks
that will not come.

april winter
mud/white
and bone chill
we stop in
tire track ankle
water hollow
to hear first
bear hoots
of spring

butterflies roost
on the new flowers—
Swedish maidens
basking in the sun

## CAT

Missak on his
rocktop moss
covered throne
(in our fern &
flower garden)
sits & catches
flies and keeps
his belly warm.

JUST NOW

the grasshopper
that leapt into the
snow-on-the-mountain
chased the white
moth out

OPENING THE DOOR AND ENTERING
THE BARNYARD, ETC.

I see
first the cock
then the 5 hens
coming,
head-high in the uncut
grass—
my little redheads

# CITY, CAT

there is a clock
in the window
that looks like a clock
ticking

the silent cat
at the tenement
window, sniffs
the noises and
alarms—stares
out the window
expressionless,
his tail anchored
to another sound.

five doves of autumn
blow past the
naked chestnut tree
seeking a hidden
bower—

the white daisies
above the sleeping cat
inhale the night

the hawthorne berries
must be ripe—
5 pigeons on the
sidewalk pecking:
4 sparrows in the
branches, knocking
them down

## HIGHER AND LOWER MATHEMATICS

Two pigeons on the stoop
    where was 3—
  1 flew down

One pigeon on the walk
    where was 4
  3 flew up

WINTER NEWS

the new november wind
is blowing summer out to sea

•

the wing-set lone seagull
floating in the sky
takes the city's pulse

•

gliding with the tide
the barge is pulling
a piece of the city
out to sea

CAT

The yellow bedspread
he sleeps upon
is slowly changing
to the gentle quiet
gold of his breath.